AF488261

PORTAL

Your Book is a Portal to the World on the Other Side

MARY GRANT

INK & IMPACT PRESS
DUBLIN, IRELAND

PORTAL

Your Book is a Portal to the World on the Other Side

Publisher: Ink & Impact Press

ISBN: 979-8-89860-621-3

Book & Cover Design: Pluto Grant @ House of Pluto Printed in the United States / United Kingdom

For founders who are ready to be fully
known for what only they can do,
the way they do it.

CONTENTS

THE PORTALS

PORTAL

Prologue

Confession. I wrote the closing note for Portal before I wrote the whole book.

I couldn't write the book I wanted to write from the version of me that was still negotiating with self-doubt and word count. I needed to write from the identity that could hold the finished version. I wasn't writing forward. I was writing back — as if the person on the other side already existed and I was simply catching up with her.

That's what a portal does. It doesn't wait for you to arrive. It pulls from the other side.

I was already into the second draft of another book when a client stopped me mid-sentence. I was talking about how his book was a portal to the world on the other side — a throwaway line while explaining why his book mattered beyond the page count. He went quiet. Then said 'That landed hard.

You should make that a whole thing.'

I laughed it off. I was neck-deep in one book already. But the idea wouldn't leave me alone.

Back tracking a little…

I've been watching something for years. Brilliant people finishing their books, holding the finished product in their hands, then asking: 'now what do I do with it?' As if the book was the end point. As if all that work, all that thinking, all that extracted genius was meant to sit on a shelf and wait to be discovered.

That question always told me something was missing. Not in their books but in how they were thinking about books.

I have always built worlds that didn't exist. From my fashion business and my stores to my role as a thinking partner and coach to high performers. I see what makes my clients a 'market of one'. We build their world around that.

I never set out to help people write books. It happened by accident when I walked a client through writing a tiny magnetic book for her business. She went from zero to number one on Amazon in six weeks. When I told that story, people started showing up asking for help to write theirs—high-calibre individuals with books stuck in their heads. People who said 'maybe someday' or had started writing, written themselves into overwhelm, and abandoned ship.

So I built a system — *Magnetic Book HQ* — to hold the process. Then one of my superpowers as a coach kicked in and raised the bar on everything. I kept meeting entrepreneurs, thought leaders, coaches with impactful book ideas that excited the hell out of me. I refused to let them dilute their brilliance. I started working with the soon-to-be authors on extracting their genius first — positioning them as a market of one before we ever touched the book.

For me, identity always comes first. The book idea comes second.

The thinking behind it is this: you're not trying to capture your entire life's work in one book. One short form book captures one impactful idea. You can have a whole series of those. Suddenly writing a book stops feeling like a life sentence and starts feeling like a deliberate move.

When people write their books this way — identity-first, genius-extracted — things start happening they don't plan for. Authority they don't have to perform. Momentum that sustains itself. Clarity that makes decisions simpler. Alignment that removes friction.

They're not writing books for those outcomes. The outcomes just appear.

Like portals.

Some portals are intentional: authority, opportunity, clients, legacy, impact, visibility. The reasons people say they want to write a book.

Some are unintentional: alignment, identity, momentum, clarity, altitude, trajectory, freedom. Bonuses that arrive as a consequence of the work itself.

That's when the portal concept refused to wait in line. This wasn't an add-on to another book. This was the starting point — the piece people need to understand before they ever begin.

How I Use This With My Authors

I always start with the world on the other side. What do you want your life to look like? How do you want to be spending your time? What do you want to stop doing, stop carrying? What lights you up? What impact do you want to have in the world? What do you want to be known for?

Now let's reverse engineer that.

When people realise the book isn't the endpoint, it's the crossing — something shifts. The ones who think of a book as 'maybe someday' start thinking: is this actually the key? They see they don't have to gather more proof or more credentials. They don't have to wait for more time. Because the book they're going to write is an intentionally short book, not a doorstop. By the time we get started, most are already thinking about a series.

Someday turns into 'how do I get this done?'.

What follows are thirteen portals. Some you'll step through on purpose. Some will open whether you planned for them or not.

I wrote the closing note first so I could write from the future version of me, not from the start line. You're about to do the same thing.

Your book is a portal to the world on the other side.

Not a someday project. A deliberate crossing that unlocks what comes next.

PORTAL

How To Use This Book

This book is built around *Thirteen Portals.*

Some you step through deliberately.

Others open because you've crossed a threshold without realising it.

The *intentional* portals are choices. They're entered with clarity and direction.

The *unintentional* portals arrive as consequences. They emerge as your identity shifts, your standards rise, and your thinking sharpens.

You don't have to read this book in order. Start wherever something pulls you.

The Intentional Portals

These portals are opened on purpose.

One will be the reason you decide to write your

book.

You may well decide you want several of them.

Authority

Visibility

Opportunity

Client

Impact

Legacy

The Unintentional Portals

These portals are thresholds that appear through movement.

These don't respond to effort. They appear as a result of writing your book.

Lean in and they all may appear.

Alignment

Clarity

Identity

Freedom

Altitude

Trajectory

Momentum

PORTAL

The Authority Portal

(Intentional portal)

Authority is claimed. Not granted.

I wrote my first book the traditional way. I thought it would take 6 months, it took eighteen. Eighteen months of focused work. The manuscript came in at thirty-five thousand words.

Then I trained for an eight-minute TEDx.

A wonderful couple who curated the event in Denver taught us how to craft a talk. They told us that TEDx talks have got shorter and shorter over the years because social media has made people's attention spans shorter. The sweet spot is now 8 minutes. We were taught how to curate a talk that holds attention. When you have eight minutes, every second matters. Every story earns its place.

Every word has to add value. Over three months of training, we cut and cut again until we could deliver our why, our message, and our authority in eight minutes. That experience changed how I think about authority and how to hold a room.

**Authority isn't created by convincing the reader.
It's created by standing still long enough for the room to adjust.**

So I rewrote that first book to go with my TEDx release. I ruthlessly applied the eight-minute thinking, giving the reader everything they needed and nothing they didn't. That was the moment something clicked for me. The power of a book written in service of the reader — not the ego of the author. A book that delivers impact and gets people taking action.

For me, a book is an authority-building artefact. But the real point is the world on the other side. That's where I start with my clients — the book is just the vehicle. I have written three books. People were coming to me every week asking for help with theirs. I didn't look around to see what anyone else was doing. I didn't let the fact that I don't identify as a book coach or a publisher stop me. I didn't wait for permission. I built a system to hold the process and got to work.

The Authority Portal opens when you decide, then plant your stake in the ground.

Authority is Gravity.

Authority is not a trophy that's handed to you. You claim it. Once you stake your claim things begin to happen. The moment your work has a spine, the energy around you shifts — It says you have nothing to prove. People can feel that. The right people meet you there.

People with true authority don't wait for permission. They just show up and claim it. There's always something in their lived experience that qualifies them to talk about the thing. Their perspective is built on what they know to be true. It's unique to them. They don't worry about gathering more proof because they know somebody has to go first — they have the courage to be that person.

Obviously, there are other people talking about exactly what you want to talk about, but they're not you. You're the only one who can do what you do the way you do it. That's your magic. You just have to claim it.

Authority doesn't need validation. It doesn't need anyone to agree. It just holds its ground.

How Authority Reveals Itself in the Book Writing Journey

When you are planting your flag in the sand, there's a moment right before it hits the ground where you catch your breath and think 'right, we're doing this!' It's the moment of no return. I see the exact moment it happens in the eyes of every client I work with. First they go still, then I catch the spark in their eyes and I know it's game on!

That's the moment you unconsciously decide to stop waiting for more knowledge, more proof or more validation. It's the moment you decide that you are just going to show up for your ideal people, sharing what you know and they need.

When I walk clients through writing their books, I always start with identity. Who are you? What do you stand for? What pisses you off? What is your contrarian point of view? What do you know to be true whether or not it's widely accepted yet?

There's a misconception that you have to have it all together before you write your book. The truth is that the version of you who starts writing, is not the one who finishes. The process of writing the book evolves you. If you start from a place of questioning whether or not you can even write a book, writing it will evolve you into the person who could. It will evolve you through new levels of identity. Writing a book will change you, in ways you never expected. Plant your flag. Then trust the journey.

The World On The Other Side

Before the book, every conversation starts a little further back than it should. You know what you know. You've done what you've done. But the context lives in your head and getting it across takes work — credentials, anecdotes and patience. You're damn good at what you do and you're still validating yourself.

After the book, that stops.

Your work hasn't changed. But now your thinking can be encountered before somebody even meets you. Conversations start pre-loaded with context. People have already spent time with your thinking. Once they have been inside your head, they are not assessing if you are worth listening to. They know you are. Now they want to go deeper.

Authority doesn't mean no one pushes back but when people disagree with you, it's cleaner. Nobody has spent as much time down the rabbit hole thinking about your topic through your lens as you and that can be felt. Disagreement is just information. People can engage with your position without it feeling personal. You are now shaping the conversation.

The authority portal is not about status. It's about orientation.

The Authority Portal Passport

If authority is one of the reasons you're writing this book, don't let your book be accidental. Plant your flag. Claim your position. Don't just share ideas or demonstrate expertise. Authority in a book doesn't come from sounding clever, qualified, or confident. It comes from deciding where you stand and refusing to wobble once you're there.

What carries you through:

A willingness to write from your actual position, not a neutralised one. Writing as though your ideal client is already listening - not the sceptics, not the people who want you to explain yourself onto safe ground, not the ones who are never going to get you anyway.

What commonly trips writers:

Softening your edge instead of bringing your full voltage. Trying to make the work agreeable. Trying to sound like you think a book should sound. Managing how you might be received —

which is a form of hiding and the fastest way to a vanilla book.

What it often feels like:

You may feel exposed, vulnerable. Like standing without cover while the words are still forming. You may feel a recalibration where you stop editing yourself for comfort.

What actually helps:

Playing full out in your writing before it feels safe. Authority firms up when you just go for it, you will integrate it along the way. Writing for authority means letting the reader feel your standards on the page. That requires not writing as if permission is required.

The version of you that starts writing is not the one who finishes. Plant your flag. Then trust the journey.

PORTAL

The Alignment Portal

(Unintentional Portal)

Being good at something can disguise the cost of carrying it.

Alignment, misalignment, alignment, misalignment, it's an endless cycle of evolution.

My most recent cycle coincided with starting to write this book. Thirty-three years running my fashion business and five years into coaching, I was holding one business in each hand and honestly, it was exhausting.

Each option had its merits. Nothing was wrong. Nothing was broken. And that's exactly where alignment becomes interesting because the real cost of misalignment shows in energy cost and sacrificing momentum to keep all the options open.

Being good at something can disguise the cost

of carrying it. Override doesn't announce itself. It sneaks in the side door. It becomes familiar… and costly. I knew that I could keep carrying both and probably do a good job at both. But I've had a big team in the past and I don't want to go there again. I knew that if I put one thing down, I could hit a home run with the other. Once that decision was made, it was easy to see which option I wanted to go all in on. The first thing I reclaimed was personal time — time that had been sucked into my fashion business when I was rebranding. I automated what was already working and stepped back. Immediately, everything felt lighter.

Alignment doesn't ask you to have everything figured out. It asks you to notice where you're getting in your own way. Where yeses are costing you in time, energy, focus, impact and fully stepping into what's next.

When The Evolution Says No

Before anything changes at a conscious level, resistance creeps up on you. It shows up in small interruptions that should take minutes but cost you direction — the quick tasks that fracture your focus. Suddenly, things that once kept you busy start to feel like nails on a chalkboard. For me this looks like emails I side-eye and don't want to open. Or requests that place demands on my spaciousness. Or people wanting to plug into my nervous system. All things I used to tolerate that now have strict boundaries.

And the bigger things, the ones that once made sense on paper that no longer feel aligned in your body. Some of my favourites: peers wanting to collaborate where there is no common thread. Customers wanting me to do a pop-up. Requests to give a day to speaking at a conference that has nothing to do with where I'm going. All things I would have said yes to in the past.... All now hard nos.

Individually, even if all the pieces are manageable — together, they start to feel like weight you no longer want to carry. Your intuition names what can't travel with you, long before your mind is ready to let it go.

Override doesn't announce itself.
It sneaks in the side door.

Momentum stalls the moment you try to continue as you were. Something has outgrown the earlier pattern. Rooms feel restricting. Opportunities that once excited you now feel off. You hesitate where you used to move without thinking. The hesitation is the signal. You stop reaching for things before you decide to stop. You're not resisting the world. You're resisting your own outdated role in it. Not everything is meant to continue.

Some Versions of You Can't Continue

The current version of you isn't the same as the evolution of you. Some elements of your identity don't belong to future you — and future you writes your book. Your evolution begins the minute you commit to moving forward.

This isn't about abandoning who you've been. It's about recognising the moment a version of you is complete. Yes, every version of you should be celebrated, every version of you brought you to where you are today. And…. some versions of you end quietly. Some end mid-sentence. Some simply stop coming with you.

When alignment takes the reins, things change internally before they ever show up in the world. Your tolerance for busyness shifts. Noise that once felt normal now feels like interference. Your decisions get made by direction, not by excitement, not by desire. Rooms feel wrong before they look wrong. It's not that you are trying to simplify — you're just no longer willing to live with mis-alignment.

This is the alignment aftermath.

How Alignment Reveals Itself in the Book Writing Journey

Writing a book unpacks your mind in ways you cannot anticipate. It becomes a mirror that reveals what moves you forward and what can't come with you. The recognition sneaks up on you, before you feel ready to name it. There are moments when you can feel previous versions of you slowing the direction you're moving toward, and you feel the tension immediately. The choice is yours, you can stay or you can move. But staying isn't neutral anymore.

A lot of the noise you are tolerating reveals itself in the process of creating your book. By nature, a tiny magnetic book demands leaving out as much as it includes, giving your reader the juice without the squeeze. Helping them to get mindset shifts that change how they see things. Your own mindset shifts happen throughout the process when you fully surrender yourself to the journey.

The World On The Other Side

Before your book, your calendar fills. Work multiplies. Life is busy and that can often be the loudest tell. Busy becomes a badge of honour. Nothing is obviously wrong. The work is fine. The opportunities are fine. And yet there's a low hum running beneath the surface. A quiet friction. You're holding multiple options open, things that create a sideways pull.

It costs more than you realise. Energy goes into things that don't really matter. Time gets spent maintaining conversations, commitments, and projects that aren't actually moving you forward. You stay in motion, but not always in the right direction.

I noticed this when I was writing this book over the Christmas holidays. I was sneaking in little writing sessions while the house was quiet. I knew it was a golden opportunity because everybody else was in holiday mode. Emails were quiet, my phone was quiet. Then January third arrived and all hell broke loose. Suddenly I was back into dealing with everybody else's demands and I could see very clearly the ones that were moving nothing forward. Not me, not even them.

While you're writing your book, something changes.

You start editing for coherence. You cut paragraphs that drag a chapter sideways. You remove ideas that don't belong to the spine of the work. You feel it immediately when something doesn't fit anymore. And that skill doesn't confine itself to the book.

After the book, that same discernment starts showing up everywhere. You notice where meetings dilute momentum. Where relationships require translation. Where projects create noise instead of movement. The things that used to feel tolerable are suddenly not. You feel it in your body before you become conscious of it. You don't need dramatic reasons to let things go. You start to shed them one at a time as you trust the clean pull forward.

Alignment makes you clearer. It's not about doing less. It's about refusing what slows down your direction. There's less internal negotiation, less self-management. From the outside it can look like confidence. From the inside it feels like relief.

Alignment doesn't ask you to have everything figured out. It asks you to get out of your own way.

PORTAL

The Clarity Portal

(Unintentional Portal)

Clarity creates capacity.

When Covid closed my fashion stores and I moved my business online, I was running the business from home. I wanted to keep it that way. Bringing in a team would have meant losing privacy or relocating the business. I wanted neither.

I almost burned the whole thing to the ground and then I paused. This was an opportunity to evolve it into exactly what I wanted. So I set myself a constraint: the business had to run in a few hours a week.

For the next six months, everything I touched was filtered through one question: *How do I make this lighter and easier?* Every single process and touchpoint was eliminated or streamlined. Overwhelm evaporated. Busy work fell away.

Four and a half days a week opened up that hadn't existed before. That's when coaching stopped being a side project and became my next chapter.

Once they were set, the constraints were non-negotiable. Customers wanted me to add things that created complexity. Even my daughter, who was helping me remotely while she was in college, suggested ideas that would have pulled the business sideways. None of them were wrong, but they would have added complexity and that was a hard no for me.

Distance does the sorting. Time does the curation.

If alignment sheds what can't come with you,

clarity creates capacity. And I was protecting my new found capacity at all costs. With clarity, the no's were clean. There was no emotional charge, no explaining, no justification.

Something interesting happened after that. The requests stopped coming. The customers didn't.

Constraint Creates Capacity

When you lean fully into a thread that feels most alive, something sharpens. Decisions stop wobbling. Spaciousness appears where overwhelm used to live.

Choosing one option to go all in on and letting the rest go cold doesn't mean erasing them forever. It means parking them for now, in a place you can return to later. And the thing is, most of what gets parked never gets revisited. Because once something else reaches heat, the need evaporates.

Distance does the sorting. Time does the

curation.

42

How Clarity Reveals Itself in the Book Writing Journey

Writing a tiny magnetic book forces a decision to follow one thread of curiosity. You can't chase everything at once. The act of writing demands concentration, long enough to reveal what's actually alive.

While you're writing, your attention turns inward. You stop scanning externally for permission, trends, or reassurance. You begin drawing from your own lived experience, pattern recognition and language that has been forming for years. No one else can assemble those pieces in the same way because no one else is inside your head.

During the writing, clarity arrives as constraint. You cannot carry every idea once the book has to hold a line. The work pushes back. Some thoughts no longer fit beside each other. Keeping them all alive stops feeling generous and starts feeling sloppy, because the work cannot support several directions without losing integrity.

While the book is being written, there's no room for side-stepping clarity. Remember the eight minute TEDx? Every decision to preserve one thing costs another. Every page that drifts becomes surplus to requirements. It takes courage to cut, even when there is friction. The work itself begins to demand reduction as a structural necessity. In the writing of this book, seventeen chapters became thirteen. 27,000 words became 16,000. Because anything that was extra was ruthlessly cut. The book knew what it needed to be. Clarity removed what was in the way.

What kept me moving forward on this book, was knowing what I wanted it to do on the other side. Knowing the impact I wanted it to have on the right people. It was as if the world on the other side was impatiently waiting for the book to be complete.

After the book, clarity becomes irreversible. Some things just no longer attach cleanly to what's most important now.

The World On The Other Side

Before the book, flashes of clarity arrive in moments. You can see the patterns. You can name what's happening. And still, a lot of directions feel possible. Openness can look like freedom but actually costs more than it gives.

After the book, your field narrows.

Certain directions simply stop making sense to pursue. Some possibilities just stop pulling on your attention. Focus isn't forced. It's a consequence of having named what matters. I still have several things I want to pursue but they are sitting on the sidelines while I work on Magnetic Book HQ.

Only time will tell if they are revisited later.

Decisions start moving faster. The question stops being '*could I?*' and becomes '*is this the right direction?*' That might seem like a subtle distinction. It's actually a distinction that collapses time. There's less circling. You're not trying to stay relatable or keep every door open. Your energy becomes more economical. Your effort stops scattering. You stop spending time in rooms you don't need to be in.

Acting on clarity doesn't make you harder. It makes you uninterested in being universally agreeable. Clarity turns awareness into direction-readiness. Even if you're not acting yet, you're no longer undecided. You just stop keeping all doors open. Certain directions simply stop making sense to pursue.

Clarity creates focus that isn't forced. It's a consequence of naming what matters.

The Identity Portal

Identity doesn't prepare you for the writing. It changes because of it.

I knew when I started this book that for it to really serve as powerfully as I knew it could, I was going to have to write it from the future version of me. The version of me at the start line did not yet have the language to pin down the swirling thoughts and ideas that needed to be captured and tamed.

When the version of you on the other side starts writing the sentences, identity begins to shift in ways you don't immediately name or justify. Somewhere in the drafting, the voice on the page outgrows the version of you who sat down to write it. You realise the person doing the writing is not the same person who had the idea. The book starts dragging you forward faster than confidence ever could.

Identity shifts arrive mid-sentence. One day you're trying to sound ready, word vomiting feral thoughts and feeling like an imposter. The next, you notice you're matching the tone of the person you're becoming without effort.

Identity doesn't prepare you for the writing. It changes because of it.

Identity Isn't Fixed. It's Activated.

Your future identity can't be conveniently pinned down before you write. It evolves and sharpens as you go. The writing doesn't just express who you are. It expands who you're becoming.

Most people think they need to have everything figured out before they can write with authority. But evolution happens through wrestling with sentences that sometimes feel like a five year old is writing them. The page doesn't require a perfect identity to step politely out of your head. It requires the willingness to evolve through the work, even when it feels really uncomfortable… especially when it feels really uncomfortable.

Identity isn't static. It moves. And it can move fast while you are writing your book.

How Identity Reveals Itself in the Book Writing Journey

There's a moment when a line lands and you feel the shift. Something becomes available to you that wasn't there before. In that moment you can feel your evolution.

Something unlocks. Words start to flow without being checked. You stop editing yourself as you go and hesitations that used to throw obstacles in your way disappear. You write something that feels like an upgrade and, without even trying, the next one follows. Each shift compounds and you feel yourself being unleashed on the page.

When you are deep into the process, you find language you didn't have access to before. Or you suddenly see a lived experience from a different perspective. Either way, the writing starts to evolve you before you realise what's happening. A sentence comes to you that you're not ready to live yet. It becomes the evidence you rise to meet.

> **A sentence comes to you that you're not ready to live yet. It becomes the evidence you rise to meet.**

The gap between who you've been and who you're becoming appears on the page before it shows up anywhere else. The writing space is private, and that matters. You get to catch up at your own pace. There's a quiet power in that — an inner knowing that feels like a secret you don't have to explain yet.

The evidence shows up in small ways. You notice you're already moving towards a new identity before you've consciously decided to. Because the discomfort happens in private, by the time you step outside, it's already integrated. The awkwardness never makes it past the drafting of your book.

At some point the writing stops requiring force. You feel settled, anchored in what you are creating. It feels like this is *yours* now, not just in the claiming of it, but because you are leaning into your own evolution.

The quiet power of writing shifts your self-image before anything else changes. People may sense that something is different, even if they can't put their finger on it.

Internally, permission stops being a requirement. You know something has already crossed a line.

The World on The Other Side

Before the book, even with clarity, negotiation is running in the background. You choose which version of you shows up in different rooms and on different occasions.

Something else happens during the writing.

You spend weeks inside your own thinking. You unpack ideas you've never sat with this deeply before. You turn them over. You question them. You refine them. Then you edit them again. And again. Your perspective gets reorganised. Your insights line up. Your internal landscape changes.

Nobody will ever give your subject the level of sustained attention you give it while writing your book. By the time it's finished, your thinking isn't theoretical anymore. It's integrated. Your ideas aren't floating around in your head. They're arranged. Held. Lived. That creates a different kind of steadiness. You're less reactive. Less easily knocked off centre. Less affected by other people's opinions because of the work you've done in private. People can feel it, even if they can't name it.

After the book, negotiation drops.

It's not that you stop caring what people think — it's that you can now be encountered without explanation. Your thinking has been documented. You're no longer the sole carrier of your own point of view.

You notice it in how you speak. You stop front-loading context. You don't feel pressure to justify where you're coming from. You're consistent across rooms and contexts. Your through-line doesn't wobble. You stop asking, *Is this on brand for me?* You start asking, *Is this true from where I stand?*

The writing process doesn't just express your identity. It expands it. You step though the identity portal with embodiment.

Your book starts dragging you forward faster than confidence ever could.

55

The Freedom Portal

Freedom isn't the reward at the end. It's the condition that allows what comes next.

When I was writing my first book '*Empowered by Style*', I created style archetypes based on what I knew to be true from studying women in my fashion business for over 20 years. Was it a proven science that I could reference? No. Was I running the risk of attack when the book was let loose in the world? *100%*

When I am speaking to something I know to be true, I visualise one specific person I am speaking to, one person for whom I know what I am saying is true.

Something shifts internally when you give

yourself full permission to speak from your truth —
something you can't get if you speak from a place of
needing approval. A willingness to hold your edge
over softening to please more people makes you
stand out from the crowd. You become magnetic to
your ideal people.

Ownership over proving

If you try to write your book for everyone,
you are speaking to nobody. Permission adds
steps. Imagined reactions add hedging. Your book
becomes something people nod to rather than lean
into.

Once you are clear on your audience and
the intent of your book, your energy can be fully
directed into creating exactly what your book needs
to deliver — everything your reader needs and
nothing they don't.

When approval stops being a constraint, a

few structural things change immediately. People pleasing disappears. You stop writing or shaping anything for an imagined evaluator. There's no internal panel to impress, no silent judge to anticipate. Your work no longer needs to land well. It just needs to land true.

Your work no longer needs to land well. It just needs to land true.

This is something I really struggled with. For a full year, I played with where my edge was and then my coach said after a difficult conversation: 'This was so clean. You are my role model for not making assumptions and not taking things personally.' In that moment, I felt something in my chest release. I let go of a fear I'd had for decades around being too direct. It was a breakthrough moment I couldn't have planned for, that came from staying in the work.

Proving requires delay. You check, you adjust, you add context. Without proving, decisions collapse into direction. This isn't about you suddenly becoming braver, it's that you are no longer negotiating. Questions shift from *'will this be accepted?'* to *'does this point to where I'm going?'*

When proving ends, justification becomes redundant. You don't pre-empt confusion or build bridges for people who aren't crossing. You stop narrating your intent. You trust that the right people will meet you. Your work stands without needing anyone's approval.

Proving, negotiating, seeking approval all burn energy upstream. When they're gone, that energy turns into precision. You make fewer, cleaner moves. You have stronger boundaries around what enters the field of consideration at all.

Freedom becomes structural. It anchors you in knowing you don't need permission to choose direction. Once that's true, everything downstream reorganises around it.

How Freedom Reveals Itself in the Book Writing Journey

When your book exists as a reference point, you're no longer the primary source. Your book holds the line for you. People don't need access to your mood, availability, or charm to understand where you stand. Your work speaks when you're not in the room. On its own, that changes how often you're pulled into explanation or defence.

Comparison loses its leverage. Your book establishes a frame that didn't exist before — *your* lens, your experience, your unique point of view. Once that's in place, other people's moves stop functioning as signals for yours. You're operating from a map — your map — not scanning the horizon.

Direction stops being hypothetical. It doesn't require defence once it's owned. Your book makes certain paths feel available and others feel irrelevant. Off-track options stop being viable. You simply withdraw your consent from things that feel like a no. Busyness thins out because fewer things qualify for action. Filling space becomes unappealing because you have reclaimed energy that you don't want to surrender again. Emotional negotiation fades. You don't need alignment meetings between your head, heart and instinct. Direction resolves all that tension upstream.

You become harder to move because you are anchored. A reference point creates gravity. Opinions don't bounce you around. Trends don't redirect you. Feedback can still inform, but it no longer displaces you. Requests sort themselves. Once a reference point exists, people approach you through it or not at all. Vague, misaligned requests don't escalate. Once your book exists, returning to ambiguity quickly reveals itself as a 'no thank you.'

When permission isn't part of the equation, decisions become quieter. Ownership stops recruiting witnesses — no announcement, justification or performance required. You decide, then move. Consistency becomes easier. Decisions start agreeing with each other because they're all coming from the same reference point.

The internal chatter stops around what will be well received or whether you should adjust. Because there's nothing left to debate. What's left is not certainty. It's steadiness.

The World On The Other Side

Before the book, even aligned work carries background pressure. To stay visible. To keep momentum going. To not let anything slip. Even when you enjoy what you're doing, there's still a sense that if you step back something important might unravel. Everything lives too close to you. If you pause, everything pauses with you.

After the book, that pressure lifts. Your work no longer depends on your constant presence to exist. Your thinking holds its shape in the world without you holding it up. Nothing collapses when you rest.

You notice it in your time first. Days stop being full by default. Space appears without guilt. You choose depth without feeling like you're disappearing from your own work. You step back and the work keeps going. Your book creates durability. People reference your work. Conversations start from it. You're not required to reinitiate your thinking for it to stay active. It's doing its job while you're elsewhere.

This kind of freedom is not about escape. We are not talking about running off to work with your laptop on a beach somewhere. This freedom is spaciousness that allows for what comes next. Freedom that allows you to relax in the mornings, or skive off for an afternoon without guilt. Once you're not juggling all the balls every day, movement becomes sustainable without burning you out.

What's left is not certainty. It's steadiness.

The Visibility Portal

(Intentional Portal)

Visibility doesn't need polish. It needs coherence.

When I joined 4PC, a mastermind for the top 4% of coaches in the world, playing with visibility was the first edge I had to navigate. I had no idea how to show up in that space. I didn't want to sit on the sidelines waiting to figure it out, so I dived right in. It was seriously uncomfortable at first. The temptation to delete posts was real. But my vibe word for the year was 'whatever' and every time I wanted to take something back, I used that word to regulate myself and moved on. After a few weeks I was able to 'post and ghost' — which to me means showing up and not be attached to what anybody thinks.

Fast forward. Halfway through the second draft of this book, I was asked to do a guest interview inside a mastermind. The book was still messy. The cleaning up had started, but a lot of the thinking was still raw. I would have preferred if the book was further along. I didn't love the idea of showing up mid-way through a creative process. It felt exposing, like revealing one of my fashion collections before the pieces had been perfected. I really wanted to say no.

People don't connect to polish.
They connect to presence.

But the mastermind leader had just completed her own book with me and she had members who were writing their books. Some insights and tips would be helpful to move them along. She didn't want rehearsed answers. She wanted an interview style. So I let go of perfection and leaned in.

She knew exactly where to probe, because she knew exactly where the juice was. As she did, my thinking flowed in real time. Not the polished version — the work that was still forming. I could feel the room shift. People weren't nodding politely. Heads were down, scribbling furiously. They were meeting the real work before it was ready. The work held, even in its raw state — I didn't need to manage how it was being received for it to land.

Visibility doesn't need polish. It needs coherence.

The Invisible Contract of Visibility

There is an invisible contract most people are inside when it comes to visibility. They didn't sign it consciously, but they live by it. It's reinforced daily by gurus promising methods that will finally make visibility easy, painless, guaranteed — and we all know that's a magic pill that still hasn't been invented. There's a quiet wanting there. A desire for visibility without friction, often paired with an allergy to being visible in the first place.

The contract says that visibility must look a certain way to count. That it requires constant output. That it demands performance and contortion. That relevance is something you earn by staying busy, responsive, and available. It keeps people chasing trends and tactics rather than choosing direction — reacting rather than standing still.

And it's exhausting. So much time and energy spent doing things outside your expertise that drain your battery and don't move the needle. It's motion disguised as traction. It's no wonder progress stalls.

When the Book Becomes the Centre

The moment your book gives the reader a stable centre to stand in, that contract begins to loosen.

Before the book, there is no denying your experience, hard-won insight, genius even. But it's disorganised genius. It lives in fragments, instincts, and conversations. Without a centre, that brilliance requires constant tending, explanation and amplification just to be understood.

Writing the book captures what previously lived in your mind and organises it in a way other people can actually use. Once that centre exists, explanation stops being something you personally have to perform over and over again. Other people can now do it for you because there is something specific to reference. You do the thinking once, and it keeps working afterwards. One to many. Amplification without depletion.

Frequency creates dependency — you have to keep feeding the machine to remain relevant. With a book — even when you're quiet — people can find your work, reference it, and pass it on without you needing to tend to it constantly. Having an asset that works for you even while you sleep starts to carry more structural weight than being seen often.

Your silence begins to do work too. A refusal to show up in ways that aren't aligned speaks volumes about where you will show up and why. You are grounded in choices that protect your freedom. By default you stop getting pulled into other people's urgency. Spaciousness is preserved by design.

Contortion, explanation, proving and performance become part of an identity that gets left behind. When you know exactly who you are speaking to, you don't need to be understood or seen by everybody. The urgency to earn attention again and again starts to feel unnecessary.

Visibility behaves differently when it serves your true direction. Authenticity becomes part of your toolkit. You feel less resistance because you're no longer wrestling with your own nature. It becomes easier to lean in and give something your energy, because that energy is reinforcing a direction you have already claimed.

Visibility from a place of power doesn't require certainty. It requires honesty. The resistance to certain forms of visibility no longer needs to be argued away or reframed as discipline. It becomes information. A signal that shows you what to ditch. And you fully lean into what feels energising instead.

How Visibility Reveals Itself in the Book Writing Journey

Visibility starts showing up while the work is still forming.

It appears as a subtle shift in how you relate to being seen. Early on, writing feels private and contained. The page is a place you can think without consequence. But somewhere in the drafting, that changes. You realise that what you're writing has edges. It would hold if you let it loose in the world.

And with that realisation comes a new kind of awareness. You become conscious of how the work might be read. A line lands and you think, 'That's going to be felt.'

That's the moment that visibility has already entered the room.

The temptation at this stage can be to manage perception in advance. To soften your language. To add context so you are not misunderstood. To make the work easier to receive. Not because it isn't true, but because it's specific. This is where many people panic and step back into performance, even while writing something meant to free them.

If you stay with the work long enough to let it integrate, instead of correcting it, something else happens.

You start to feel where the magnetic core of the book actually is. Which lines carry weight? Which ones could be deleted and not be missed? The page becomes a mirror. You can tell when you're writing from your centre and when you're writing to people please.

As your book develops a spine, your relationship with being seen changes again. You stop thinking about visibility as something you need to generate and start experiencing it as something the work itself will carry. The writing no longer feels like exposure. You're putting a message out there rather than yourself. And that makes all the difference.

By the time the manuscript has real structure, visibility has already reorganised itself. You can tell when a sentence is anchored, and when it's reaching. That shift makes you steadier.

Visibility anchors when the writing no longer tries to manage being seen. The Visibility Portal opens when the work becomes recognisable to the people it's actually meant for.

The World On The Other Side

Before the book, being seen takes effort. You plan it. You schedule it. You wonder if you're saying enough, often enough, in the right places. Visibility depends on activity. When you go quiet, you disappear.

After the book, your ideal people can spend an hour in your thinking and know you're exactly who they've been looking for.

Recognition arrives before you do. Your name carries context. People reference your work before they've met you. Conversations assume familiarity with how you see things. Introductions are shorter because a lot of the introducing has already happened.

Your book makes visibility more efficient. You don't need to be everywhere. One coherent expression travels further than constant broadcasting, because everything is recognisably yours and the more you it is the better. The work circulates without you escorting it.

Visibility stops feeling performative. You're not managing perception anymore. You're allowing orientation. The right people find you when what you stand for is relevant to them. You become their obvious choice when they're ready.

The visibility portal is presence in the field that keeps working when you're not.

The Visibility Portal Passport

If visibility is one of the reasons you're writing your book, you need to be intentional about how you show up, not just *that* you show up. Bring all of you, the power, the fire, the humour, everything that makes you *you*.

What carries you through:
Writing to one specific reader and letting the rela-

tionship be direct. The book needs to speak from a stable centre that doesn't need you to perform or prove. Visibility comes from clarity of your position.

What commonly trips writers:

Becoming self-conscious mid-flow. Hiding behind the work, not letting the real you show up on the page. Editing your voice for fear of being too much. Trying to pre-manage how the work will be received rather than letting it stand on its own.

What it often feels like:

Clenching. Sudden panic about how the work might be received. The instinct to soften edges, to add disclaimers, to make the work more agreeable.

What actually helps:

Remembering that no one can see the work while it's emerging.

Immersing yourself fully in the process so you get to the deepest layers of you. Letting the raw extraction of your genius flow and evolve. The book knows where it's going once it's allowed to flow.

Visibility isn't created by managing perception —
it's created by standing still long enough for your
work to find the people it's meant for.

*The visibility portal opens when your work
becomes recognisable to the people it's
actually meant for.*

PORTAL

The Client Portal

(Intentional Portal)

Clients move when they recognise themselves in your work.

When I wrote my first book Empowered by Style, I ventured into territory that felt brave for a fashion book at the time. I was introducing ideas that sat left of centre, and I wasn't sure how they'd land.

My customers recognised something in what I'd written, something that was bubbling beneath the surface but hadn't yet been named. The book changed how they shopped, They started buying less and better. Contrary to what you might expect, that deepened their loyalty to my brand because it introduced a new way of thinking.

That book kicked off my first coaching venture, which I ran for four years. I taught women how to evolve through different stages of life using their wardrobes. How to show up unapologetically as the best version of themselves. Women from all walks of life, from stay at home mums to women in powerful leadership positions told me that the work we did changed their lives. Because it changed their self-image.

When I closed that membership to focus on coaching in the business space, I didn't want the work to go to waste. So, I created a free version of it. Today it's available free to any woman who wants it. People sign up every day. A lot of them go on to be customers of my fashion brand.

It's About Resonance

When your book is focused on client first, it starts behaving like a place people arrive in rather than a pitch they respond to. Someone reads a line and feels seen. Someone else reaches the end of a paragraph and thinks 'I know who to talk to now.' Clients show up because they see themselves between the lines — stepping closer feels safe.

Your book filters before you ever speak to someone. When a reader opens your book and sees their own thinking reflected back, something shifts. They don't need more information. They just need to know they are in the right place.

Recognition invites movement. It sparks curiosity about what might be possible that they haven't yet encountered. For the right people, that creates a magnetic pull.

When people feel seen in your work they don't need to be sold. They just come closer.

Let Them Meet You

Your readers want to know you, the real you.

Let them see you. Let them feel you.

They want to be inside your head. They are not looking for the polished version of you, or the version you think is permitted. They want the you who notices what others miss, who thinks deeper than the surface answer, who cares enough to choose truth over perfection.

A book doesn't sell your services. It pre-qualifies the relationship.

Your book creates that pull when you bring humanity, lived experience, vulnerability, and your unique lens. Your readers see glimpses of themselves in what you've lived through. If humanity is not present, the relationship cannot deepen.

That first book *Empowered by Style* opened with me sharing my own moment of lost identity. When I hit my fortieth birthday, I didn't know who the hell I was outside of being a mum and business owner. It was an embarrassing admission for somebody who worked in the fashion industry. People connected with it because it happens to every woman somewhere along the line. Life throws her a curveball side-swipes her confidence — whether it's a big birthday, a test from the universe or just being the person who gives to everyone else before looking after herself.

Perfection creates distance. Humanity, vulnerability and unfiltered truth draw people closer— the kind of clean truth that comes from lived experience. The scars of battles won and lost.

Reveal Your Lens, Not Your Perfection

Your readers are not looking for the cleanest journey. They connect with someone who understands how the journey feels. Your lens is the bridge — the way you interpret, decode, and translate experience. Your lived perspective is the atmosphere they are stepping into. If they like how it feels, they'll come closer — and in my experience stay for years.

When you create something from a place of not looking for approval, it can absolutely feel risky. And that's often where standout work lives — where you lean into what you know to be true, before validation. The greatest rewards come when risk is involved.

Your book filters before you ever speak. The most powerful books don't try to please everyone. They let the wrong people walk on by without confrontation or apology. Every person who recognises 'not for me' clears the path for one who whispers 'I think I've found exactly what I need.'

How the Client Portal Reveals Itself in the Book Writing Journey

A truly impactful book doesn't sell your services. It pre-qualifies the relationship. Potential clients choose how you see, how you think, how you move through problems. Your book makes that visible before you ever speak.

Embracing that you are not for everybody is not risky. It's liberating. When that knowing drops from your head into your body, you bring a different kind of energy. One that can get fully behind your book's mission. Being unfiltered is not reckless. Absent of emotion, it's clean energy, where there is no residue and nothing to argue with. Your reader is either in or they are out. And both are ok.

You might be thinking: But what if someone uses my ideas without being a customer? The truth is, they will. There will be readers who DIY everything. Some people will always choose the stairs over the elevator. And, you get to choose what to share and what to keep behind closed doors.

You might be thinking: *But what if someone steals my ideas?* Believe me, I have lived this one many times over in my fashion business. Yes, they will. But they cannot copy your thinking or the version of you that writes the book. They can copy where you've been … but not where you're going.

The World On The Other Side

Before the book, potential clients arrive curious but as yet, uncommitted. They want to understand what you do, test whether you're a fit, decide if they trust you enough. Conversations spend time circling context. You're translating your value in real time, reading the room as you go.

After the book, clients arrive pre-oriented.

The book acts like a filter and a magnet at the

same time. Your name starts travelling with a reason attached. The book does some of the introducing when you're not in the room. By the time someone reaches out, the conversation has already started. They've already been inside your thinking. They are already half way down the road.

By the time they contact you, the decision is mostly made. The conversation isn't about convincing anymore. They're past *'can you help me?'* and into *'what happens now?'*

The work itself moves differently too. Less time spent orienting. More time spent applying. Less resistance, because the initial decision was better informed.

Client relationships become cleaner because they begin from shared language, shared beliefs, shared direction.

Clients don't arrive to be persuaded. They arrive aligned.

The Client Portal Passport

If the Client Portal is one of the reasons you are writing your book, you cannot hide behind ideas. Let them meet you fully. Let them see your values, your beliefs, your quirks, your intolerances. These all build trust and bonding.

The commitment here is relational. You are not writing a book to demonstrate competence. You are writing a book to allow the right people to recognise themselves in your presence and decide they want to move closer. That only happens if you let your way of thinking come through on the page.

What carries you through:

Commitment to speaking directly to the person your book is truly for. Speaking from inside the work, not preaching from the balcony. Letting the reader see the real you, the human that they would connect with if they were sitting across the table having a conversation with you.

What commonly trips writers:

Using impact as a reason to stay broad. Writing in a way that offends no one and therefore reaches no one fully.

What it often feels like:

Discomfort. A sense of excluding people who might otherwise approve.

What actually helps:

Accepting that some readers will fall away. Precision is not a failure of generosity. It's what allows the work to land with the people you actually want to reach.

Before you write, you need to decide:

How do I want the reader to experience me in this book. What would it feel like to sit across from me? Am I writing as an instructor, or as someone in conversation?

If your book is meant to act as a Client Portal, it cannot just read like an instruction manual. It needs to read like a relationship forming in real time.

Every person who thinks 'not for me', clears the path for one who thinks 'I think I've found exactly what I need.

93

The Opportunity Portal

Opportunity follows clear direction.

I had a really uncomfortable moment a while back. My coach asked me a question and I squirmed in my seat. Are you willing to be known as 'The Queen of Magnetic Books'? I froze.

One of the hardest things to do is to let go of all the options and go all in on one. I've seen it with all of my clients and I'm right there with them. That moment where you think 'but what if I pick the wrong thing'.

She pressed me on it because we were working on a game plan that needed me to commit to a specific offer — even though I have several strings to my bow. So, she reframed the question: 'Are you willing to be known as the queen of magnetic books for the next 12 months?' Different question……

I looked in the rearview mirror and saw all the unplanned pivots, the things that worked … and then didn't. The times I changed direction and everything was okay. I relaxed. In that moment, I mentally parked a few things I want to create. I was in — committed to Magnetic Book HQ — for 12 months.

Once I committed, I could see exactly what I needed to do next. It felt like being at the start of an open runway, revving up the engines.

Within two weeks, three people approached me to collaborate.

Openness Repels

Keeping options open feels smart right up until it becomes a hiding place. At first it looks like agility, curiosity, strategic patience. But there comes a moment where the openness stops serving your next level of success.

There's a particular kind of openness that repels the rooms worth being in. The kind that says 'I'm available to anything … therefore I'm anchored to nothing.' People can't place you. They can't refer you for the panel, the podcast, the partnership. They don't know who you belong alongside. The invitation never forms because the shape of you hasn't been made undeniable yet.

Competence keeps you in circulation. Worldview determines where you get invited in.

Staying broad looks like flexibility. In practice it weakens your signal. Every conversation starts from scratch. Every introduction requires a backstory.

The right rooms fill up while you're still figuring out how to describe yourself.

Direction is gravity. A line in the sand is not a prison. It's a signal. Without a signal, opportunity has nowhere to land.

Direction Attracts

When direction isn't named, everything stays hypothetical. People might sense that you're capable. They might even admire what you do. Admiration can certainly get you invited to many things.

And a clear direction creates discernment around what's actually right for you. What becomes possible once a direction is declared, even imperfectly, is that you become referable. Someone can say, 'Oh. That's what he/she's for'. It gives them language. It gives them a way to speak about you when you're not in the room. Without that, even well-intentioned people can't put you forward for the right stage, collaboration, or introduction in the right moment. They like you. They just can't place you.

The invitations most aligned for you don't come from just being impressive. They come from being placeable. Someone needs to be able to imagine your name in a specific context — on a panel, in a room, alongside other people moving in the same direction — and feel certain it belongs there.

Direction needs to be inhabited. Opportunity responds to occupancy. Someone standing somewhere, even shakily, is easier to invite than someone hovering convincingly everywhere. The moment you commit to a direction, a different kind of conversation becomes possible. Not 'what do you do?' but 'You should talk to…' or 'We're building something and I immediately thought of you.'

That's the shift. From explaining yourself to being circulated.

The Cost of the Wrong Room

Every opportunity you say yes to carries an energetic cost in the delivery. Not just time in your calendar, but the invisible load: context switching, emotional presence, recovery, recalibration. The wrong rooms require you to go down rabbit holes that are not of your choosing but that serve somebody else's agenda.

A client asked me three years in a row to speak at a conference that she organises. My talk was to be the wild card in an otherwise very serious event. I said yes because I didn't think I could keep saying no to such a good client. It took two days of my time to build the talk and another two days at an event that was not in alignment with my direction. Being in the wrong place does not feel disastrous in the moment but it comes at the cost of something else not moving forward.

When nothing is allowed to self-select out, everything becomes a candidate. Invitations from people who want a version of you that doesn't quite exist. Collaborations that require you to curate yourself. Platforms that put you in front of an audience that's not quite yours. You show up. You do it well. And you come away feeling vaguely off-course.

The cost isn't just time. It's trajectory. Every wrong room you occupy delays the right one finding you. It sends a signal that you're available for that — which brings more of that. Direction does the filtering that effort never can.

Meaningful opportunity excludes more than it includes. It excludes activities, but it also excludes interpretations of you. It closes down who people think you are available to be for them. No explanations or justifications required. It's either aligned or it's not.

Your Lens Is the Invitation

Competence is abundant. Plenty of people can do the work well. Competence answers the question: can you do this?

Worldview answers a different question: should this be done, this way, and why?

The collaborations worth having, the platforms worth appearing on, the rooms worth being in — they aren't trying to fill a skills gap. They're trying to advance a direction, a conversation, a way of seeing the world that needs allies, not just operators.

Resonance bypasses comparison. When your worldview is visible and specific, people don't shop around. They recognise something in the way you see the world that matches the direction they're moving in. Trust forms faster than evidence when you're clearly playing the same game.
Competence keeps you in circulation. Worldview determines where you get invited in.

Chasing vs Organising

Chasing opportunity reverses the relationship. The moment you chase, you move into appeal mode. When you are chasing, you adjust your pace, mirror the room, people please so nothing feels uncomfortable. Yes becomes the default because it feels risky to say no. The bar quietly lowers.

Aligned opportunity prefers pace to speed. It needs coherence, enough consistency to recognise itself. When opportunity is allowed to organise itself around what is aligned, something subtle but powerful shifts. You stop arriving in rooms and start being sent for. People connect your name to ideas without your involvement. Invitations arrive already shaped, for something specific, from someone who already understands your lens.

Curating opportunity isn't disappearing. It's consolidating. It feels quieter. Fewer threads but stronger pull. That's often when people panic and think something's wrong. And then they pause and think 'oh hang on, this is what freedom actually tastes like'. Clarity is doing the work effort used to do.

How the Opportunity Portal Reveals Itself in the Book Writing Journey

A book written without a clear direction can still be good. It can even do well. What it can't do is circulate with intent.

When a book is written from a clear position and points toward a specific future, it starts doing something most authors don't anticipate. It becomes a reference. Someone reads it on a plane and mentions it at a dinner. Someone uses a phrase from it in a pitch. Someone gives it to a colleague before a meeting because 'this is the frame we're working inside'. The book travels. It carries your thinking into rooms you haven't stepped into yet. And in those rooms, it opens doors.

The invitations that follow a well-directed book are different in kind. The podcast host who found you through a mutual contact who quoted your book in a meeting. The collaboration that forms because someone read two chapters and immediately knew there was a shared agenda. The stage invitation that arrives because your thinking landed in the right room.

This requires a specific kind of writing discipline. Not just writing what you know, but writing toward what you're building. Allowing your ambition to be visible on the page. Naming the future you're moving toward, not just documenting the ground you've already covered. The book needs to be legible not only as a record of expertise but as a signal of direction.

When intention is dialled in upstream, your book behaves differently. Stories get sharper. The through-line becomes visible. The book stops being something you created and starts being something that creates opportunities for you.

The World On The Other Side

Before the book, opportunity arrives as a maybe. Conversations are exploratory. You're often asked to introduce yourself, establish context, make the case before anything real can happen. The gap between 'I'd be interested' and 'let's move forward' is wide.

After the book, that gap closes.

Your name starts travelling with a reason attached. The book introduces you when you're not in the room. Opportunities stop arriving as loose enquiries and start showing up with shape. Someone has already read your work. They know the frame you operate from. They arrive ready.

Scale becomes possible because your thinking is in more places than you are. Ideas compound. Influence circulates. Doors open that you didn't knock on — because someone else recognised a connection you couldn't have predicted.

The opportunity portal isn't about volume. It's about trajectory — shifting you from available to referenceable. From capable to circulating.

The Opportunity Portal Passport

If opportunity is one of the reasons you're writing your book, you are committing to write from direction, not from availability. This portal does not open just because you are visible, or impressive. It opens when the book makes you undeniable.

The commitment here is trajectory.

As you write, you are choosing to anchor the book in to the future, not the past. That means writing with enough ambition that others can imagine building alongside it. A book that is too contained, too cautious, or too self-referential has nothing for opportunity to attach itself to.

What carries you through:

A very clear intention for the book, paired with the courage to write it playing full out. Allowing your worldview, standards, and direction to be felt on the page without apology.

What commonly trips writers:

Prioritising breadth over depth. Keeping edges fuzzy in an attempt to stay universally appealing. Writing as though the goal is to offend no one rather than to be recognised by someone.

What it often feels like:

Pressure to hedge. A temptation to soften or generalise 'just in case'. A worry that committing to one direction will close down others. It won't. Specificity opens unexpected doors. Vagueness quietly closes them.

What actually helps:

Writing decisively and expansively at the same time. Being ruthless about what belongs in the book and what doesn't. Opportunity emerges from precision carried with conviction. The right invitations don't come from sameness. They come from people recognising that the way you see the world creates space for something bigger than yourself.

Opportunity begins to organise itself around the clarity you put into the world, when you are willing to stop writing as though you are asking to be chosen and start writing as though you are moving no matter who's coming with you or not.

A line in the sand is not a prison. It's a signal. Without a signal, opportunity has nowhere to land.

The Altitude Portal

**Altitude isn't a place you visit.
It's a place you occupy.**

I recently took a six month sabbatical. I'd love to say that I was swanning around having coffee and chilling out. I wasn't. It was strategic time out from being on the hamster wheel to focus on the bigger picture.

I'm always telling my clients to get in the helicopter and zoom out so they can get perspective. I spent a lot of that six months in my helicopter. Zoomed out, I get perspective that I cannot get when I'm on the ground getting things done.

When the sabbatical was over, I relaunched my fashion brand and got dragged right back into the weeds. There were so many elements to tend to in that first season. I had my hands on everything and I was freaking out. This was not where I wanted to be.

That's when I realised altitude isn't a place you visit, it's a place you occupy.

Once you've operated from altitude, dropping back down isn't neutral. You lose clarity. You lose your line of sight to the bigger vision. You get swallowed by day to day busyness. That loss is impossible to ignore and being in the weeds is no longer an option.

When Direction Matters, Busyness Does Not Equal Momentum

Once direction is clear, busyness starts to feel different. Movement in different directions slows you down. Some people call it chasing shiny things, I call it chasing rabbits. Something catches your attention, sounds interesting, feels energising, and off you go. The cost isn't obvious at first, especially if you're someone with a lot of energy. Motion still feels clean. Output still looks strong. You're not struggling, so it feels like nothing is wrong.

But energy is finite and everything you say yes to has an energy cost. Once direction sharpens, that becomes impossible to ignore. Movement even slightly out of alignment starts to show up as an energy drain. Nothing compounds. You stay busy, capable, impressive even. But altitude is something that's visited instead of occupied.

High energy masks this longer than most. You can outrun the consequences and call it momentum. Until you know exactly where you're going. Then every sideways sprint becomes visible. And costly.

The Shift From The Weeds

Once you've spent any stretch of time operating

from your highest altitude, anything that drags you into the weeds starts to irritate in a very specific way. Like your calendar is hijacked by a to do list rather than creating progress towards a north star mission. Or choosing chaos over structure…ugh.

The work itself isn't a problem. It's the realisation that consent that serves other people's agendas quietly taxes your own direction. Tasks, requests, problems you once tolerated begin to reveal themselves as what slow you down — keeping you busy, stealing your focus, blurring your bigger vision. The busy-being-busy badge of honour only works until you've tasted something cleaner. After that, tolerance feels heavy.

Staying in the Helicopter

The air is cleaner at altitude. There's less noise, less rush, more spaciousness, more bandwidth.

From altitude, problems look different. On the

ground, every problem steals your time and energy. At altitude, you clearly see what's not worth your energy.

Decisions made from the ground are influenced by everything that's happening at that level. They reinforce where you already are.

Decisions made from altitude are directional. They reinforce where you are going.

The Quiet Weight of Custodianship

Once you have a clear direction, custodianship appears. You realise that where you stand now matters beyond you. Something is being stabilised by your position. When you move, it moves. Now, dropping altitude doesn't feel humble. It feels negligent.

Custodianship is quieter than leadership. It's holding a standard of thinking, a clarity of direction, a field where others orient themselves, or a body of work that doesn't yet exist fully, but is already shaping decisions. This was the piece that was sacrificed when relaunching my fashion brand took all my attention. When altitude dropped, I lost my clarity of direction. That was a cost I wasn't prepared to pay.

The altitude portal opens when urgency loses its authority, when what once felt complex simplifies into priority. From altitude, decisions don't feel heavy. They feel clean. You're no longer choosing between options. You're choosing from clarity.

Altitude isn't a place you visit. It's a place you occupy.

How Altitude Reveals Itself in the Book Writing Journey

In writing, altitude shows up the moment you start writing toward what actually matters. Early drafts begin close to the ground. You're inside the work. Inside the stories. Inside the context. Brain dumping everything that seems relevant, which is exactly what you need in the early stages — that's how you mine for the gold. Then something shifts.

Altitude is where authority settles

You notice yourself pausing before including things that once felt essential because they are surplus. A story might be true, but it doesn't serve the direction. A concept might be clever, but it pulls the work sideways. You instinctively feel the difference between relevance and importance in your body.

Altitude shows up as editing without resentment. You cut things you like. You leave out things you could explain beautifully. You stop rescuing the reader from discomfort or confusion because you can see what they actually need or don't. Your writing becomes more deliberate. You're no longer responding to imagined questions from ground level. You're bringing exactly what is needed with full potency.

When words are fewer but weightier, I often see people panicking — thinking they need more words, more explanation, more proof. But that urge pulls you downward. When you stay at altitude, something else happens. The book starts organising itself. Threads converge. Decisions become obvious. What stays in needs no justification. What gets left out is no longer debated. What at one stage feels like something you're assembling, starts feeling like something you're revealing.

Altitude is where authority settles.

The World on The Other Side

Before the book, you're close to everything. Decisions, conversations, requests, problems arrive at ground level. You're reacting to what's nearest or loudest. Patterns are hard to see when you're inside them.

After the book, your operating altitude changes.

Writing the book required you to step back far enough to see what connects, what repeats, the through lines, what's actually driving outcomes. That distance doesn't disappear once the book is finished. You don't drop back to your old height.

Altitude becomes your new baseline. A baseline you do not want to surrender.

You notice it in decisions. You recognise misalignment faster. Something either fits the bigger picture you've articulated or it doesn't.

You notice it in conversations. You stop getting pulled into micro-drama. You're less reactive because you can see where things sit in the wider landscape. You're not above people. You can just see from a zoomed out viewpoint.

You notice it in work. Busyness loses its appeal. You can feel when something is absorbing energy without moving anything that matters. The intolerance you feel isn't arrogance, it's perspective.

In relation to the writing, altitude shows up as orientation. The book becomes a vantage point you can return to. It reminds you what matters, what connects, and what doesn't belong anymore. You're not constantly recalibrating from ground level.

Altitude isn't about being detached. It's about having enough distance to choose deliberately. And once you've operated from that height, it holds. You can move into detail when needed, but you're no longer trapped there.

Once you've operated from altitude, dropping back down isn't neutral. You lose clarity. You lose sight of the bigger vision.

The Trajectory Portal

(Unintentional Portal)

Trajectory begins with a clear line of vision.

The first iteration of my coaching business started during covid. I had run a few wardrobe challenges after the launch of my first book. When everyone was in lockdown, customers asked me to run those challenges again. So, I did. Afterwards, people wanted a way to stay connected, so, I created a self-coaching society.

But, I had a bigger vision for my coaching and if coaching was to be my next identity threshold, there could be no ambiguity around what I do. For almost 30 years, I had been known as a fashion designer. So, I already had work to do!

I knew I wanted to work with founders, entrepreneurs and thought leaders, catapulting them to their next level of success while creating simplicity and freedom. Months before I had the heart to close the self-coaching society, I knew it was the next right move. So, while I loved every single one of my members, at the end of 2023, I reluctantly closed it to focus on my bigger vision.

Trajectory is not speed. It's inevitability.

Things felt quiet the first few weeks. There was no more creating content, no more showing up for weekly live events. There was a quiet ache of missing people I had shared a journey with for the previous four years.

But, I stepped into 2024 knowing what I

wanted to be known for. Standing at the start line, I could see the north star. I had a vision. I also had no idea how long it would take me to create or how I was going to get there. I didn't even know what the first step was.

It should have felt scary. All I felt was anticipation.

Trajectory Is What Remains After You Stop Renegotiating

Trajectory is not speed. It's inevitability.

Where altitude gives you the vertical lift, trajectory is what happens next — forward motion with direction, even if the destination isn't fully visible yet. You don't need the whole map. You only need to know which directions are no longer available. Your choices begin to compound, not through effort but through alignment.

Trajectory comes from removing sideways motion. Detours have nowhere to hide. Decisions feel either directionally correct or not.

Trajectory is refusal. Refusal to renegotiate actions that belong to an expired operating system. Refusal to keep explaining yourself to people who benefited from the old version of you. Refusal to treat clarity like a suggestion. Fidelity towards your bigger vision overrides people pleasing.

Fidelity looks like energy going to the same few places. From the outside, it can look like you've gone quiet. From the inside, it feels clean. There's less drag, less noise, more spaciousness. Fidelity shows up as routine and routine is where trajectory holds. Trajectory that comes from fidelity looks boring from the outside. It's unimpressive until time passes. Then the distance travelled becomes undeniable.

How Trajectory Reveals Itself in the Book Writing Journey

As your book takes shape, some things start getting left behind. Because trajectory clarifies what is no longer necessary. The shifts you encounter while writing your book start layering. You can feel the direction the book is pulling you in. Trajectory shows up as a consequence of the writing itself. Direction holds and behaviour follows. Trajectory carries you forward when enthusiasm has left the room.

The World On The Other Side

Before the book, movement is busy without being laser focused on direction. Opportunities feel adjacent. Decisions are made one at a time, each one isolated from the last. Progress exists but it's negotiable — a little faster here, a little slower there, a sideways detour that makes enough sense in the moment.

After the book, trajectory asserts itself.

You've articulated a position. You've committed to a way of seeing things. Your choices start behaving differently because direction is established. Certain options quietly drop away. Others feel inevitable.

Decisions start compounding. Each one adds to the line that's already been drawn. There's less negotiating with each move. Even pauses feel purposeful. Not every question pulls on your attention anymore. Not every invite requires a decision.

Questions that used to ask 'should we?' turn into 'how far do we take this?' Conversations move more because there's a clear through-line. Energy follows the direction without persuasion.

Trajectory happens when choices stop being isolated and start behaving like a system.

The Momentum Portal

(Unintentional Portal)

Momentum isn't discipline, it's rhythm.

Standing at the start line I knew that I couldn't write this book forward. To write the book that wanted to be written, I knew I had to write it from a future version of me. There were so many moments in the first few chapters where I thought *'I don't even know if I can do this!'*

Then about four or five chapters into the shitty first draft, I started to notice a shift. Less doubt and more embracing a new level of thinking were unfolding. As I got further in, I was more demanding of myself. I was holding the intent ruthlessly. I was rambling less.

By the time the first draft was complete, a new

level was integrating. Going from first to final draft felt effortless, almost like *is this really allowed?*.

None of this is because of any weird kind of genius — it was purely from following the vision and letting it pull me forward.

The Momentum Myth

People talk about momentum as if it's something you generate. 'Let's get in momentum.' Like it's a state you enter through force of will or a motivational talk you give yourself before the big push. Momentum doesn't ask what it will take to keep going. That question belongs to effort.

Once something is in motion, gathering momentum, continuation is no longer an act of will.

I've observed the same pattern— in my own journey writing this book and in my clients' journeys — something happens midway through the first draft where the pull takes over. People who were dipping in once a week for a couple of hours start to clear space. Because now the book is moving and they want to capture what is unfolding. Where previously I had to encourage people to give a little more time, now they are dipping into personal time because the book just won't leave them alone.

Momentum kicks in when rhythm replaces motivation.

That's the moment effort isn't required to get going. The work isn't being driven anymore — it's already moving. Your role shifts from getting motivated to moving with what's already in motion. You won't feel momentum at the start. You feel it when stopping feels harder than continuing.

Momentum holds when time away doesn't create a recovery phase. You don't come back to inertia. You don't have to rebuild belief, energy, or orientation before movement resumes. The first step back in is a step forward, not a restart.

How Momentum Reveals Itself in the Book Writing Journey

Momentum arrives when something starts moving and doesn't wait for your permission.

In the early stages of writing, everything feels chosen. You decide when to sit down. You decide what to work on. You decide whether to continue or stop. Progress depends on initiation. If you pause, the work pauses with you. Then, at some point, that changes.

You realise you're no longer choosing to write. You're responding to something that's already forming. Ideas arrive uninvited. Connections show up between writing sessions. Chapters start pulling on each other. *'Should I keep going?'* turns into *'Can I keep up?'*

When momentum kicks in, stopping feels disruptive, like interrupting something that's organising itself. The work has mass now. It carries itself forward and you're moving with it. You'll notice it when you return to the page more easily than you leave it. Breaks don't create resistance. Restarting doesn't require a warm-up.

The book stops being something you're pushing uphill. Writing stops being an act of discipline and becomes an act of response.

The World On The Other Side

Before the book, progress depends on effort. You generate it. You sustain it. If attention shifts, things slow. If energy dips, things stop. Momentum is something you create — which means when you're not creating it, it doesn't exist.

After the book, it works differently.

The book is foundational in a way that most tools aren't. You've done the thinking at scale. You have a north star that you don't have to keep locating. You've had all the secret arguments with yourself. What used to require a decision now just requires a direction-check.

Your work keeps moving when your attention moves elsewhere. Conversations keep unfolding. Ideas keep being applied. You're not re-initiating the same thinking. When you're tempted to say yes to the wrong thing, the book filters. When urgency tries to override what actually matters, the book orients. You don't have to hold all of this yourself anymore. It's been externalised. The book does the work.

Once your thinking has mass outside you, you stop generating motion from scratch. You respond to something that's already moving. The work pulls you forward rather than needing to be pushed.

The book stops being a boulder you are pushing uphill and starts taking on a life of its own.

PORTAL

The Impact Portal

Impact begins the moment your work shifts how someone thinks — and you never even hear about it.

One of the most impactful chapters in my book Magnetic Female Entrepreneur was only two pages long — a chapter that was added when the book was almost finished.

I was amazed at the number of people who shared that my 'One Degree Pivot' chapter was exactly what they needed. One almost throw-away moment that gave a lot of people an alternative perspective when they were standing at the threshold of a new chapter — when they were contemplating burning something to the ground.

Another moment that stands out for me was from my first book. A woman in a senior leadership role told me that my style archetypes helped her to shed a version of herself that belonged to a previous life. She didn't realise how much that old version of her, staring at her every time she opened her closet, was holding her back. She completely reinvented herself and has evolved to new heights in her career.

These are just a couple of the impactful moments that have found their way back to me. Tiny moments that met somebody exactly where they were at.

Impact Begins Quietly

The moment your book leaves your hands, it starts forming private relationships.

It meets people in moments you never imagined when you wrote it. A sentence crafted from one context lands in another. A paragraph intended as orientation becomes permission. A question meant to provoke becomes reassurance.

And there's anonymity. The most meaningful impact often happens where there's no feedback loop. A quiet shift in someone's internal posture. A decision made differently. Courage they borrowed. Moments you'll never know about.

Not every outcome returns to you.
And that's the whole point.

A reader can return to the same page years later and find a different doorway waiting. They see something they didn't see before because it's exactly what they need in that moment. Your book becomes a mirror with depth. Each pass reveals a slightly different angle, a layer that wasn't visible before. And yes, that includes the author. You can read your own book at different stages of your life and feel it speak back to you in a way it didn't while you were writing it. You see the same things from a different perspective.

Impact here isn't reach or reaction, it's resonance — the ability of the work to keep offering insight without being fixed to a single moment, interpretation, or state of mind. An impactful book doesn't demand to be understood in one way. It allows itself to be met differently, again and again.

Meaning Lands Where Your Strategy Can't Reach

Impact happens when a sentence slips into someone's inner monologue and starts standing in for a thought they used to have. It becomes a new default. Someone is about to respond the old way and doesn't. The script they used to reach for isn't there anymore. They see something in a different way and the game changes. They don't necessarily know why. Something else has taken its place. That's impact doing its job.

This is why you don't hear about it. There's nothing to report. No 'this changed my life' email. A person who now moves through something with a slightly different internal posture than before. And it's exactly the kind of impact that doesn't need you in the room.

Your book creates access. Your work enters conversations you were never invited to. Rooms you will never be in. Contexts where your name doesn't even need to come up for your work to matter.

Not Every Outcome Returns to You. And That's The Point

There's an internal recalibration that's required to stop managing your book once it's in the world. Trust that the roots you plant are enough. That your framing, integrity, and intent will hold. That readers will meet the work where they are and take what they need, even if it's not the thing you thought they would.

There is a very real satisfaction in knowing that your book can shift something for somebody you'll never meet. A private decision — a moment where they choose differently and no one ever knows there was even a choice to be made. It's rewarding in a way that recognition, feedback, or success can never be.

Not every outcome returns to you. And that's the whole point.

How Impact Reveals Itself in the Book Writing Journey

Putting your work into writing stabilises it. Your message stops shape-shifting depending on the room. It has a spine, a form. The work no longer depends on you to exist intact. You're not carrying it in your body anymore. It's anchored.

The moment during the writing where your work becomes external, it's no longer responsive to your micro-corrections or real-time calibration. You've been the container while the work was forming. Publishing ends that role. The work now has edges of its own.

You surrender control as you release it into the world. You give up being the one who gets to decide what the book is for in every moment. You also give up the comfort of relevance. The quiet reassurance that the impact passes through you personally.

When Ego Wobbles

Most people want their ideas to spread. Fewer have sat with what it feels like when they actually do. A book crossing into the world asks the author to shift from creator to witness. And that can feel disorienting when part of your identity has been wrapped around being the carrier of the work.

There's a perfectly human ego moment that catches you off guard the first time it happens. You hear your words or ideas reflected back to you without attribution. They have been integrated by somebody else who speaks them back to you not knowing that they actually came from you. And for a split second you feel protective of your work before you can let it go. Because being de-centred can feel, for a second, like being erased. It's a flicker and it passes.

Then something more adult steps in. Your perspective widens. You remember why you wanted impact in the first place. It wasn't for admiration. It was for movement, change, a ripple effect you don't have to supervise. That shift is subtle but important. You realise that wanting impact without examining what it actually asks of you is where most people get stuck. They want the effect, not the release. The outcome, but not the handover.

Once that lands, the ego relaxes. It stops needing to be the star of the show and becomes quietly proud of the work standing on its own two feet.

The World On The Other Side

Before the book, impact is traceable. You speak, someone hears, something shifts. The line between cause and effect is short enough to see. You know who was changed, roughly when, roughly why.

After the book, that changes.

Your thinking enters systems you'll never observe, shaping decisions you weren't consulted on. It travels through and between people. A sentence becomes a reference point. A distinction becomes a lens. A framing quietly replaces another and something evolves.

This is influence in circulation — your impact has stopped being relational. It has become ecological. Your work doesn't move to people anymore. It moves through them. It changes how they interpret situations, how they name things, how they choose. Incremental changes that ripple outwards — without any big announcement.

Someone makes a cleaner call because your thinking reorganised something for them months before. Someone else tolerates less because a line stayed with them. Or somebody passes an idea on — stripped of origin but intact in essence. This is impact without attribution — change that doesn't require your participation.

And this is where you underestimate what you've actually done. Because the work doesn't just affect individuals. It affects patterns. Over time, that's how culture shifts — not through persuasion but through replacement.

Your book doesn't need to be remembered to be effective. It just needs to be used.

The Impact Portal Passport

If you are writing a book for impact, you need to be ready to let your ideas loose in the world. To not be attached to them being attributed to you or see a return on your investment. The impact portal opens when you allow the work to move on its own terms. When you trust that what you created is enough to carry forward without supervision. And to know that the rewards will show up in ways you didn't anticipate.

What carries you through:

Acceptance that your work will move without you.

What commonly trips writers:

Trying to monitor, manage, or measure impact too closely. Looking for immediate evidence that it worked.

What it often feels like:

A strange silence. The book is finished, the

effect is mostly invisible. Influence begins privately, without feedback loops.

What actually helps:

Letting the work form its own relationships. Impact isn't performance. It's consequence. The book does its work in places you will never see, and that's the whole point.

Your book stops being about you and starts doing it's work in the world.

The Legacy Portal

(Intentional Portal)

Legacy isn't about remembering. It's about evolution.

I had an aunt, a coach before her time. Two years before she died, I asked her if she would write a book. She said no. She was in the process of shredding her notes. My heart sank. For her, an act of love, making life easier for her kids when she was gone. It never even occurred to her that her wisdom could be the starting point for somebody else. The cost — the work that she did over a lifetime came to a full stop.

For many years I have thought about what it would be like to download our wisdom on the way out of this world, instead of taking it with us. It's one of my motivations behind helping powerful people to get their genius out of their heads and into the world.

When we leave the world with our genius trapped in our heads, evolution stops. Hard earned wisdom. Lessons learned. Patterns revealed. If they leave this world in somebody's head they are lost. Somebody else starts from scratch.

Legacy Is Not Just a Parting Gift

The trouble is that too often legacy is seen as a final someday thing. Which in itself is a tragedy because there is so much genius unfolding in the heads of amazing people, genius that does not have to be fully formed to be unleashed.

You can develop your thinking faster and farther once it's outside your head. It becomes way more powerful from the input of those you gather around you. Too many people wait for the right time. They think it's not fully formed yet. They haven't worked it all the way through.

What if instead the whole point is to unleash it into the world without having it tied up in a bow. An open-ended thing that hits the world like a live wire.

Legacy isn't just what you leave behind. It's what keeps working because you let it evolve outside your head.

That's where stewardship comes in.

Ownership says this is mine to defend. Stewardship says this is mine to tend and let go.

A steward doesn't control how the work is received. They don't curate agreement. They don't wait until the environment feels friendly. Their responsibility is to ensure the work is clear enough, honest enough, and strong enough to stand on its own feet once it's placed.

And yes, that includes allowing challenge, criticism, friction. These are not side effects, they are part of the job. If the work matters, it will be met. If it's met, it will be tested. If it's tested, it will be sharpened or discarded. That's not failure, it's the magic.

Stewardship asks a harder question than ownership ever does. Not 'will they like this?' but 'does this belong in the world now?' And once the answer is yes, the responsibility is to act, not to manage the aftermath. Letting the work go doesn't mean you abandon it. It means you trust it enough to let it have a life beyond your supervision. You stop gripping, translating, sanding off the edges so no one feels uncomfortable.

I have spoken to so many powerful people who say 'I'll write a book someday.' People who think they have more to learn, more to gather, more to prove. They think of writing a book as unpacking your whole life's work. It's no wonder it's a 'someday' goal.

And then I plant the seed of a tiny book. One book, one idea. Not your whole life's work. One thing that can create an impact now — in the time it takes the reader to have a leisurely lunch. A lot of people decide to move on the spot, even more circle back within a week or two and say 'let's do it'.

A decision to move creates legacy because it creates contact, which creates consequence. And consequence is the only thing that matters.

That's the responsibility. Not to be right but to place what you're entrusted with when it's alive, even if it's not yet fully formed.

How Legacy Reveals Itself in the Book Writing Journey

A book does something lived experience can't do on its own: it stabilises meaning.

You're taking something that lives intuitively in your body and translating it into a form someone else can navigate. Without structure, people can feel the impact of your work, but they can't orient themselves inside it. They might borrow a moment. They might carry a feeling. They might quote a line. But they don't get the architecture.

A book makes the architecture visible.

It lets someone see the full terrain rather than stumbling across landmarks. It shows how ideas relate to each other, not just how they land in isolation. It creates a shared map, so people aren't left reverse-engineering your thinking from scraps.

Lived experience disappears when you're not there. A book holds the through-line. It preserves how you think. The order you place things in. The sequence you believe matters. The logic beneath the intuition. That's what lived experience alone can't mobilise. It's too dependent on proximity. A book makes your thinking portable without distortion.

When your work is captured in your book, it stops being a private mental loop and becomes a shared object. We are not talking about a mystical version of legacy. This is mechanical stewardship.

Legacy shouldn't wait for completion. Because completion is a solo act.

Once it's placed, even unfinished, your expertise becomes something others can respond to rather than something you have to carry alone. People don't just add ideas. They test it. They interpret it. They extend it. They see edges you can't see from the inside. They apply it to contexts you'd never think to design for.

Legacy shouldn't wait for completion because

completion is a solo act. Legacy requires exposure to thrive and grow. When people gather around the work, it no longer depends on your internal coherence alone. It gains structure through use. It is shaped through friction. Direction evolves through response. Movement changes the trajectory far earlier than refining in your head ever could.

The World On The Other Side

Before your book, legacy is abstract. A maybe someday aspiration. Something that other people might assess in hindsight. The idea of being remembered lives vaguely, somewhere in the future, out of your hands.

After the book, legacy becomes concrete.

Your thinking has been given a form that can endure — be returned to, built on, argued with, passed along. It no longer depends on your memory, your reputation, or your continued presence to exist. It stands on its own.

You notice it when people who've never met you are shaped by the work. When your ideas continue to inform decisions long after the original context has changed. When what you put out into the world becomes part of the background architecture — a foundation that other things get built on.

In relation to writing, legacy shows up as longevity. The book stays relevant because it captured something structural, not timely. It holds its meaning as circumstances shift. People don't just discover it — they rediscover it at different times, it speaks to them for different reasons.

Your role changes when your book hits the world. You're not trying to extend your reach. You're tending to what you want to remain true and allowing the world to make contact and evolve it how it needs to.

The legacy portal is not about remembering, it's about evolution.

The Legacy Portal Passport

When you know that time doesn't create legacy, decisions do, you stop outsourcing meaning to someday. You realise nothing matures just because you waited. It matures because you let the world meet it.

What carries you through:
A decision to place your work while it's alive, not archive it for someday.

What commonly trips writers:
Treating legacy as a final act. Waiting until the thinking feels complete or safe to share.

What it often feels like:
Responsibility. A sense that placing this work now matters more than perfecting it someday.

What actually helps:

Recognising that legacy is created through decision, not time. Writing now doesn't pretend to capture everything you'll ever know. It places what matters enough to carry forward. Influence begins the moment your work is released.

Ownership says this is mine to defend. Stewardship says this is mine to tend and let go.

PORTAL

Afterword

I knew writing this book would be a climb. The person who started would not be the person who finished. I had to let go of pleasing, over-explaining, rescuing. I had to write it from inside the process so the reader could feel the journey and recognise the thresholds. It was hard. For the first five chapters, I wasn't sure I could do it. Then I got in rhythm.

I wanted it to be like an eight-minute TEDx that leaves you changed without dragging you through the autobiography of how the insight arrived. A book you could read in an hour or two and feel something shift.

It was simple. It wasn't easy.

Writing short takes courage. It takes ruthless subtraction. It's harder to write less than more. It's harder to choose what gets left out. It's harder to cut the clever lines that made you feel safe because they proved you knew something. It's harder to stop explaining and stand in exposure.

I wrote this book in three weeks. Not because it was easy — because years of thinking came first, and the system I use with my clients held the process. My first draft was double what you're holding. I cut and cut and cut again. To make it laser focused.

I didn't want this to be a book that performs authority. I wanted it to stand in it. This is the identity it took.

Being:
The one who stops waiting to feel ready.

The one who doesn't add 30,000 words to look serious.

The one who understands that clarity is proof enough.

The one who believes a book isn't big because it's long — it's big because it moves something.

If you felt something here — a pull, a doorway, a slight ache of recognition — you're already standing near your own version of this. You don't need to earn the right. You don't need more evidence. You don't need to wait until you've lived an entire second life to talk about the one you're in.

Choose where you want to stand.

Then write from there, not towards it.

The length will take care of itself.

You might recognise yourself here:

Your next level is calling you forward...
you just haven't fully claimed it yet.

Your work is having a real impact...
but you keep telling yourself you need a bit
more proof.
A bit more clarity.
Something more before you claim it fully.

You're successful. You're busy.
And your energy is spread across too many
directions.

You've narrowed your focus...
but you're still holding back from planting
your flag.

You know exactly what you're here to do...
and something in you is saying: *now*.

**If one of these landed... you'll already know what
to do next.**

What's Next?

Your book is already forming.
It just needs a portal.

One idea.
One tiny book.
Let's build it.

hello@marygrant.com

www.marygrant.com

Also by
Mary Grant

Unleash Your Inner Goddess

The Magnetic Female Entrepreneur

AFTERWORD

Mary Grant is an entrepreneur, designer, and Authority Architect who helps impact-driven founders build a world around what they want to be known for.

She works with founders who are already in motion, helping them define the one idea their work stands on and build the authority, assets, and visibility around it — so they become a market of one.

Multi-award-winning entrepreneur, TEDx speaker, and founder of Magnetic Book HQ — where high-performers extract their genius and unleash it into the world.